Did you hear about the hillbilly who passed away and left his estate in trust for his bereaved widow?
(See page 7)

How can you tell the mother-in-law at a Jewish wedding?
(See page 23)

What song did the mermaid sing to the sailors?
(See page 39)

How come they took John Wayne Toilet Paper off the market?
(See page 52)

What's the first thing a sorority girl does in the morning?
(See page 67)

What's the difference between your paycheck and your wife?
(See page 104)

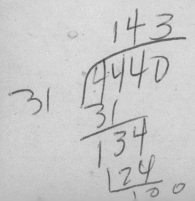

Also by Blanche Knott
Published by St. Martin's Press

TRULY TASTELESS JOKES IV
TRULY TASTELESS JOKES V
TRULY TASTELESS JOKES VI
TRULY TASTELESS JOKES VII
TRULY TASTELESS JOKES VIII
TRULY TASTELESS JOKES IX
TRULY TASTELESS JOKES X
TRULY TASTELESS ANATOMY JOKES
TRULY TASTELESS ANATOMY JOKES II
TRULY TASTELESS DOCTOR JOKES
TRULY TASTELESS LAWYER JOKES
TRULY TASTELESS MILITARY JOKES
BLANCHE KNOTT'S BOOK OF TRULY TASTELESS ETIQUETTE
THE WORST OF TRULY TASTELESS JOKES (HARDCOVER)
THE TRULY TASTELESS JOKE-A-DATE BOOK

Blanche Knott's

Truly Tasteless Jokes XI

SMP
ST. MARTIN'S PAPERBACKS

TRULY TASTELESS JOKES XI

ISBN: 0-312-92619-7

Printed in the United States of America

St. Martin's Paperbacks edition/November 1991

10 9 8 7 6 5 4 3 2 1

for Jarratt,
to help you stay
in the public eye

CONTENTS

ETHNIC VARIEGATED

Why do Canadians like to do it doggie style?
So they can both watch the hockey game.

•

Miss DeAngelo was a none-too-bright Italian girl who had moved to Hollywood with dreams of becoming a star. She didn't find fame or glory, but she did encounter plenty of men willing to enjoy her plentiful charms, and eventually she found herself named in a divorce case.

When it was her turn on the stand, the prosecutor came forward. "Miss DeAngelo, the wife of the defendant has identified you as the 'other woman' in her husband's life. Now, do you admit that you went to the PriceRite Motel with this Mr. Evans?"

"Well, yes," acknowledged Miss DeAngelo with a sniff, "but I couldn't help it."

"Couldn't help it?" asked the lawyer derisively. "How's that?"

"Mr. Evans deceived me."

"Exactly what do you mean?"

"See, when we signed in," she explained, "he told the motel clerk I was his wife."

•

Why did the Mexicans fight so hard to win the battle of the Alamo?

They wanted a wall to write on.

•

When Liam decided it was time for his friend Brendan to part with his virginity, he accompanied him to the local whorehouse and explained Brendan's condition to the madam. "Don't worry, my boy, we'll get a nice lass to take care of ye," she promised. "Ye just do your part and make sure ye wear one of these." And the madam took a condom out of her drawer and rolled it down over her thumb by way of instruction.

Brendan parted eagerly with his money and bounded up the stairs to Room Twelve, where a cheerful farm girl soon showed him the ropes. After he'd come, a frown passed over her face. "The rubber must have torn," she muttered. "I'm wet as the sea inside."

"Oh no it didn't, Miss," Brendan cheerfully reassured her, holding up his thumb as evidence. "It's good as new."

•

To Brazilians, the only person stupider than someone Portuguese is a Brazilian politician. So they tell the one about the Portuguese man who had an appointment with the Brazilian senator:

The senator had been kept waiting for hours when the Portuguese emissary finally arrived, sputtering with apologies and explanations. "Where the hell've you been?" roared the Brazilian.

"I know I'm terribly late, but it wasn't my fault," protested the visitor meekly. "I reached your office building with time to spare, but then the escalator broke down and it took them forever to repair it. Why, I had to stand there for almost two hours."

"What an imbecile!" bellowed the senator, turning red in the face. "What a moron! You're telling me you *stood* on that escalator for *two hours* while it was being fixed?"

"Why, yes I did," replied the Portuguese.

"You idiot! Why didn't you *sit down*!?!"

•

Why did they have to cancel both the sex education and drivers ed programs in rural Mexico?

The donkeys couldn't handle it.

•

Two white guys and a dark Puerto Rican found themselves up on the roof of the apartment building on a hot summer day. "Man, you should check this out," said one of them to the Puerto Rican, stepping up onto the parapet. "The wind really whips off the river around this building. Look." And he jumped off into space, plummeting for a few stories, then catching an updraft and floating gracefully to the sidewalk below like an autumn leaf.

Watching the maneuver in astonishment, the Puerto Rican guy gasped in admiration. Then, crossing himself, he took a flying leap off the building, only to splatter onto the street a few seconds later.

Surveying the gruesome spectacle, the other white guy ruefully shook his head. "What a racist asshole," he murmured. "That Clark Kent just can't stand Puerto Ricans."

•

Did you hear about the two Italian restaurateurs who decided to go into business together?

One morning Sandro was the first one into the office. Right away he called his partner to scream, "Gino, we've been robbed!"

"Sandro," ordered Gino sternly, "put the money back."

•

Why was Bunker Hill slimy?

"The British are coming! The British are coming!"

•

The bitter Anatolian winter was almost over when one Armenian shepherd turned to the other and confessed that he could hardly wait until it was time to shear their flocks.

The other shepherd nodded, rubbing his hands together in anticipation. "It's great selling the wool in the market and spending some of the money on raki and women, eh?"

"That's not it," said his companion. "I just can't WAIT to see them naked!"

•

Spinelli was called in as a witness in a bloody Mafia assassination attempt. Determined to take a hard line, the presiding judge was unpersuaded by his opening testimony. "Did you or did you not see the shot fired in the restaurant?" the judge demanded.

"I'ma no see da bullet, but I'ma hear it fine, like I jus' tol' you."

"That is not satisfactory," pronounced the judge. "Step down." The witness obeyed, but started to laugh as he turned away and headed off the stand. The magistrate proceeded to berate him for his conduct.

"You Honna," asked Spinelli, "you-a see me laugh?"

"I've got ears, don't I?" roared the judge.

"Atsa no satisfactory."

•

How many canaries can you get under a Scotsman's kilt?

Depends how long the perch is.

•

Anatoly was watching the May Day parade in Moscow with his friend Yevgeny. He beamed with patriotic fervor as one hundred ultra-modern tanks rumbled through Red Square, flushed with pride as crack battalions bristling with Kalashnikov rifles marched by in precise formation, then scratched his head in puzzlement: the next group to pass consisted of ten men in rumpled grey business suits.

Finally he tugged on Yevgeny's arm. "I understand the tanks, the soldiers, the guns and missiles. But what's with those ten men?"

"Those, my friend, are economists," explained his friend. "Have you any idea how dangerous ten economists can be?"

•

What do you get when you cross an African-American and a goat?

A lawn mower that doesn't work.

•

How do you get twelve Mexicans out of a phone booth?

Throw in a bar of soap.

•

Jean-Pierre and Luigi decided to go hunting together. They trekked deep into the woods, set up camp, and headed out the next morning in search of deer, when what should run across the clearing in front of them but a lovely blonde, stark naked.

"Oooh la la," sighed the Frenchman, smacking his lips, already missing the fair sex. *"Mon Dieu,* but how I would like to eat that delectable creature."

So the Italian took aim and shot her.

•

Did you hear about the hillbilly who passed away and left his estate in trust for his bereaved widow?

She can't touch it till she's fourteen.

•

Ibn Saud ben Alekh, a respectable and dignified merchant, was attending a camel auction in the main square when he was overcome by the most terrible intestinal cramps. Finally, unable to contain himself, he let out a giant fart, which was so noisy and so pungent that the people around him looked aghast and stepped back in a circle.

Overcome with shame, Ibn Saud went straight home, packed, and turned his back on his birthplace. For many years he led a nomadic life, wandering from town to town, but as old age approached, so did the longing to return to his hometown. By this time he was aged and stooped, his hair and beard as long as the Prophet's, and his confidence grew that no one would recognize him and link him to that mortifying moment.

So he returned to the town and headed straight for the main square, where he immediately noticed that the mosque now boasted a spectacular turquoise and gold-leaf facade. Turning to a passerby, he commented on the magnificent mural. "In the name of Allah," asked the old man, "can you tell me when it was completed?"

"Let me think," replied the man. "Yes, that would be seven years, five months, and twenty-two days after Ibn Saud ben Alekh cut that big fart in the square."

•

How many Irishmen does it take to change a light bulb?

Two. One to hold the bulb and the other to drink until the room spins.

•

The Indian made his little fire atop a butte in Nevada and was busy sending smoke signals to the rest of his tribe when a huge explosion was heard from the nearby atomic testing ground. A spectacular mushroom cloud rose high into the sky.

"Geez," muttered the Indian, "now why couldn't *I* have said that?"

•

How do you sink an Irish submarine?

Knock on the door.

•

The Ecuadorian captain had grown increasingly anxious over rumors of an impending air strike from neighboring Peru. "Pedro," he ordered his aide-de-camp, "I want you to climb that mountain and report any signs of Peruvian military activity."

"Si, Capitano," replied Pedro. He trudged up the mountain, and as soon as he crossed the ridge he saw a squadron of planes heading their way. "There are many planes coming, Capitano," he promptly radioed back.

"Friends or enemies?" the Captain demanded urgently.

Pedro again lifted his binoculars to the sky. "They're flying very closely together, Capitano," he replied. "I think they must be friends."

•

It was two days before Christmas, so the Irishman had to fight his way through the crowd at the Heathrow check-in counter to inquire, "How long does it take to fly to Dublin?"

The harried clerk glanced up. "Just a minute, sir."

"Thank you so much," said the Irishman, turning away.

•

What do you get when you cross a fat person from China with a can of Campbells?

Chunky soup.

•

Judge Lipsky was presiding over a case of insurance fraud in which millions of dollars were at stake and which had taken almost a year to come to trial, and she was especially eager that matters proceed without a hitch. So she was appalled when the court convened on the fourth day and the jury box held only eleven people. "And where is the twelfth member of the jury?" she inquired briskly of the foreman.

"Well, Your Honor, it's St. Patrick's Day, as you may know. The missing man is Brendan O'Rourke, and he'd never pass up marching in the parade. But don't worry—he left his verdict with me!"

•

The prostitute was quite impressed when her Chinese client took her up to his room in the swanky Hotel Crillon, where they screwed for quite a while, until he rolled off, gasping for breath. *"Pardonnez-moi, Mademoiselle, je suis fatigué,"* he explained, and went into the bathroom to freshen up. When he returned, she was even more impressed by his jumping on her for a second energetic round of sex. After a while, though, he lay back on the bed, sighing, *"Pardonnez-moi, Mademoiselle, je suis fatigué."* Off he went to the bathroom again, and again returned revived and ready for another session of lovemaking.

About the sixth time around, the hooker was so tired she excused herself for a bathroom break. And when she pulled back the curtain, there were five other Chinamen hiding in the shower.

•

Mrs. Hildebrand instructed each of her second graders to use the word "choo-choo" in a sentence.

Little Jennifer said, "The choo-choo pulled into the station right on schedule."

Little Leroy said, "De choo-choo be goin' too fast."

Little Jose said, "You touch my Chevy an' I'll choo-choo."

•

O'Flaherty was brought to trial on the charge of brewing and selling his own whiskey. His lawyer had the defendant brought before the jury, and asked them to examine carefully the bleary, red-nosed, pot-bellied, ill-smelling fellow who stood unsteadily in front of them.

"Ladies and gentlemen," the lawyer concluded after a few minutes, "you have had time to look Mr. O'Flaherty over with great care. Examine your consciences, please, and tell me whether you honestly believe that if that man had a quart of whiskey, he would be capable of selling it?"

O'Flaherty was acquitted.

•

"I'm sorry, Mr. Alvarez," apologized the warden as he unlocked the soon-to-be-ex-convict's cell. "I'm afraid we inadvertently incarcerated you for an extra month."

"Don' worry 'bout it," said the cheerful if none-too-bright felon. "Jes' take it off the next time."

•

The Governor made room on his busy calendar to hear the pleas of one Señora Rodriguez that her husband be released from the state penitentiary. "What was he sentenced for?" asked the Governor gently.

"For stealing a loaf of bread," replied the offender's wife, nervously fingering her mantilla.

"Is he such a good husband?"

"No," she replied frankly, blushing a bit. "He beats me when he gets drunk, he bullies our children, he's unfaithful, and really not much good at all."

"It sounds to me as though you're better off without him," said the Governor. "Why on earth do you want him out of jail?"

"Well," she explained, "we're out of bread again."

POLISH

Did you hear about the Pole who went out to the outhouse, put one leg in each hole, and shat in his pants?

•

How about the Polish streaker?
He went through the School for the Blind.

•

How about the well-endowed Polish streaker?
He leaves three tracks.

•

How do you sink a Polish ship?
Put it in water.

Did you hear about the Polish daredevil named Evel Kowalski?

He jumped over twelve motorcycles in a bus.

•

If a Welshman and a Pole were standing on top of a tower, how could you tell them apart?

A Welshman would never throw crumbs to helicopters.

•

Why did the Polish law student fail his bar exam?

He thought an antitrust suit was a chastity belt.

•

A Pole married an American Indian, and when their child was born, what do you think they named him?

Running Dumb.

•

The Polish rocket went up right on schedule—one hundred feet . . . two hundred feet . . . three hundred feet . . .

—and then it ran out of coal.

•

How can you identify Polish tanks?
They're the only ones with backup lights.

•

What do you call a Pole who chases garbage trucks?
The galloping gourmet.

•

Why do Poles have broad shoulders and broad heads?
Because when you ask them a question [shrug your shoulders] they shrug their shoulders, and when you tell them the answer [slap the top of your head] they slap the top of their heads and say, "Christ, why didn't I think of that?"

•

Know why it takes twenty Polish farmers to milk a cow?
Two hold the teats while the others gently lift the cow up and down, up and down, up and down. . . .

•

Do you know why there's no zoo in Hamtramck?
They haven't raised enough money yet to build a fence around the town.

•

Why does it take more than four hours to get one basement window cleaned in Warsaw?

Well, it takes at least three and a half hours to dig a hole for the window-washer's ladder. . . .

•

Why did the Polish man invent the wheelbarrow?

So he could learn to walk on his hind legs.

•

What's the definition of a level-headed Polack?

One with shit coming out of both ears at the same time.

•

"Can you believe my Ignatz bought me a washer and dryer for Christmas?" boasted Mrs. Dasciewicz to her next-door neighbor. "Yes, that's right—a douche bag and a towel."

•

What's Preparation H?

Toothpaste for Poles.

•

Did you hear about the first Polish space mission? The launch went off without a hitch, the astronauts reached orbit, and the first astronaut left the capsule to walk in space. When he knocked on the door to be let back in, the other astronaut asked, "Who's there?"

•

What did they call the first Pole ever to take a bath?
A ring leader.

•

So how d'you get a Pole out of the bathtub?
Turn on the water.

•

Judge: "The charge is the theft of sixteen radios. Are you the defendant?" Polish Defendant: "No sir. I'm the guy that stole the radios."

•

Doctors don't circumcise Poles anymore. . . .
They realized they were throwing away the best part.

•

How can you tell Santa Claus is Polish?
Who else would wear that silly red suit?

•

What's the difference between a Pole and a hypodermic needle?
None. They're both a pain in the ass.

•

Why did the Pole ask everyone to save their burned-out light bulbs?
He needed them for the darkroom he was building.

•

The little Polish boy ran into the kitchen where his mother was baking a cake and cried, "Mommy, please can I lick the bowl?"

"Forget it," she snapped. "Flush it like everyone else does."

•

"For God's sake, Mary," said the old woman consolingly to her old Polish friend, "why are you weeping so? It can't be that bad."

"My husband's out shooting crap," she confessed with a sob, "and I don't know how to cook it."

•

Why do crows fly upside-down over Poland?
It isn't worth shitting on.

•

Did you hear about the Polish girl who thought a tail assembly . . .
. . . was the company picnic?

•

Why do little Polish girls always walk in the middle of the road?
They're afraid of the wildflowers in the ditches.

•

Did you hear about the Polish skydiver?
He missed Earth.

•

Did you hear about the Pole who went ice fishing and brought home one hundred pounds of ice?
His wife died trying to cook it.

•

How can you tell which motorcycle belongs to the Pole?
It's the one with the training wheels.

•

How about the Polish tricycle?
It's the one with the kickstand.

•

Why are there no fly swatters in Poland?
It's against the law to kill the national bird.

•

Why was the Polish farmer busy driving a steam roller over his fields?
He wanted to grow mashed potatoes.

•

Where did the two Polish guys go to buy a new truck?
To McDonalds, to buy a big Mack.

•

Did you hear about the adventurous Pole who got a zebra for a pet?
He named it Spot.

•

Can you figure out why Poland's going to declare war on the United States in about fifteen years?

That's when they're going to start understanding these jokes.

JEWISH

What's the difference between a Jew and an elephant?
Elephants eventually forget.

•

How can you tell the mother-in-law at a Jewish wedding?
She's the one on her hands and knees picking up the rice.

•

Nussbaum the peddler was busted for selling woolen hats without a license, and found himself hauled into court along with three prostitutes who had been arraigned on the same day. "It's all a case of mistaken identity," protested the first streetwalker to be summoned before the bench. "I'm mindin' my own business when this car pulls up—"

"Drop it," interrupted the judge. "I've seen you in this

courthouse at least a dozen times before. That'll be a hundred and fifty dollars, and it'll be twice that if I set eyes on you again. Next!"

The second hooker whined, "I was just on my way to correspondence class, Judge, to learn how to make an honest dollar, when—"

"Cut the crap," the magistrate broke in. "Two hundred and fifty bucks or ten days in jail—you choose. Next!"

The third woman came forward and declared, "Your Honor, I plead guilty: I'm a prostitute. It's not the living I'd choose, but it's the only way I can make enough to feed and clothe my family, so it's what I do."

The Judge smiled. "Finally, someone who realizes a courtroom is a place to tell the truth. To reward your honesty, young woman, I'm dismissing your case. In fact, Mr. O'Brien"—he turned and summoned the bailiff—"make sure Miss Cardoza gets seventy-five dollars from the Policemen's Benevolent Fund. Next?"

Up stepped Nussbaum the peddler, who had been paying close attention. "Your Honor," he said frankly, "I'm not gonna lie to you either. I'm a prostitute."

•

What's a Jewish 10?

A JAP with a million dollars in the bank.

•

Why aren't Jewish mothers attacked by sharks?

Professional courtesy.

•

Levin was a notorious tightwad, and alleviated his few twinges of conscience by giving a quarter to the miserable-looking woman who sold bagels from a pushcart on the corner by his office. He never bought a bagel, having already breakfasted, but he always put a quarter into her grimy palm and felt himself a virtuous man.

This went on for months, until one day the bagel-seller tugged at his immaculate cuff. "Mister, Mister, I gotta tell ya somethin'."

"Ah," acknowledged Levin with a gracious smile, "I suppose you wish to know why I give you a quarter every day but never take the bagel?"

"Nah, that's yer business," she snorted. "My business is tellin' ya the price's gone up to thirty-five cents."

•

Why was Moses' mother so happy?

She not only had fun in bed, she made a prophet.

•

What did the Jewish-mother bank teller say to her customers?

"You never write, you never call, you only visit when you need money."

•

When Selma answered her phone, it happened to be an obscene phone call. The man on the other end began describing in detail all the kinky, perverted sexual acts he wanted to engage in with her.

"Now hang on, wait just a minute," Selma interrupted. "All this you know from me just saying hello?"

•

What did the Jewish mother ask her daughter when she learned she'd had an affair?

"Who catered it?"

AFRICAN-AMERICAN

What do seven-foot African-American basketball players do in the off-season?

Go to the movies and sit in front of you!

•

When the telephone rang at the Tuscaloosa office of the NAACP the receptionist happened to be in the bathroom, so the general administrator answered the call.

"Good mawnin' boy," drawled the voice at the other end of the line. "I want you to put me through to the head nigger, on the double, y'heah?"

The administrator was understandably outraged. "How dare you talk to me like that? No one has the right, whoever they are, do you understand?"

"Calm down, boy," said the man on the phone. "I've got two million bucks that I figure might get your Martin Luther King Center finished and fixtured, and I figgered the head nigger might want to discuss the donation a bit beforehand, see? Now put me through."

"Yas*suh,* boss," gulped the administrator. "I see dat jigaboo comin' through de doah dis minute!"

•

Why was the African-American acquitted of the rape charge on grounds of temporary insanity?

Because when he got an erection, there was no blood left to flow to his brain.

•

What do you call Mike Tyson with no arms and no legs?

"Yo, nigger!"

•

What do African-Americans and sperm have in common?

Only one in two million does any real work.

•

What do you call an African-American baby smurf?

A smiglet.

•

What do you call an African-American smurf with nuts?
A smickers.

•

Trying desperately to establish the reliability and good character of his witness, the public defender asked, "Johnson, tell us, is your widowed mother dependent on you?"

"She sure is," replied Johnson with a big smile. "Why, if I didn't go pick up the washing and bring it home to her, the old lady'd starve to death."

•

Why did Michael Jackson decide he might as well be a woman?

His dick is only ten inches long.

•

Miss Struthers asked her fifth graders to name the most important invention in the history of the world. "Yes, Luanne," she began, pointing at a little girl in the front row.

"The plane, Miss Struthers," she replied. "Now people can travel really far, really easily and fast."

"Yes, Billy?" The teacher nodded at a little boy who suggested the telephone. "It makes it so people from all over the world can talk to each other."

"Very good, Billy."

"Miss Struthers, I know, I know!" The teacher looked with some surprise to a little African-American kid in the back row who was waving his arm and jumping up and down in his seat.

"Yes, Marcus? Go ahead."

"It's the thermos, Miss Struthers. It keeps hot things hot and cold things cold—and how do it know?"

•

The poor African-American boy from Macon, Georgia, felt a wave of panic come over him as he surveyed the all-white jury in the New Hampshire courthouse. Positive he'd never beat the murder rap, he managed to get hold of one of the kindlier-looking jurors, and bribe her with his life savings to go for a manslaughter verdict.

Sure enough, at the close of the trial the jury declared him guilty of manslaughter. Tears of gratitude welling up in his eyes, the young man had a moment with the juror before being led off to prison. "Thank you, thank you—how'd you do it?"

"It wasn't easy," she admitted. "They all wanted to acquit you."

•

Know why so many African-American men have started getting flat-top haircuts?

So they can balance a bucket of Kentucky Fried Chicken on their heads and still mug people.

•

Why did the ape commit suicide?

It learned it might have evolved from the native Africans.

•

Why's an African-American government worker like a shotgun with a broken firing pin?

It won't work and you can't fire it.

•

Did you hear about the ad for BMWs in *Ebony*?

It says, "You've got the radio—now get the car."

WASP

Over lunch one day Goldfarb and Allessio were discussing whether or not WASPs could be said to have a sense of humor. Goldfarb staunchly maintained they didn't. "After all," he pointed out, "why does a WASP even need one?"

"Not so," protested Allessio. "My WASP acquaintances always laugh at my jokes. In fact, I get three laughs out of 'em: once when they hear the joke, once when I explain it, and the third when they understand it."

•

"I really don't think you spend enough time with Thaddeus Junior," chastised Mrs. Carrington. "Between the office and the club, the only time you set eyes on him is when Nanny brings him in before bedtime."

Carrington shrugged and reached for *The Wall Street Journal.*

Undeterred, she went on. "I really do think you might make time next week to take Thad to the zoo."

"Certainly not," said the busy dad. "If the zoo wants him, they can come and get him."

•

"We have a new baby at our house," reported Spencer to Chandler at tumbling class.

"Neat! Is it a boy or a girl?"

"I don't know," admitted Spencer. "They haven't dressed it yet."

•

Lives of considerable privilege had accustomed Chauncey and Skiff to getting their own way, and this attitude accompanied them on a trip to Europe following their graduation from Princeton. After lunch in a little brasserie on the Rive Gauche, Chauncey snapped his fingers for *l'addition,* and when Skiff got back from the men's room, Chauncey was scowling at the bill and yelling at the cowering waitress. "I think the waitress is shortchanging me," he explained, "but I can't understand a damn thing she says. Can you believe she can't speak English? *You* took French at Andover, Skiff—help me out, won't you?"

Skiff strode over to confront the waitress. *"Parlez-vous français, Mademoiselle?"* he asked.

"Oui, oui, Monsieur," she answered in evident relief.

"Well then," he demanded, "why the hell won't you give my pal here the right change?"

•

Forman died and went to Heaven, where she was gratified to be given a tour of the place by the Angel Gabriel, who wanted to make sure she felt at home. "We have all types here," he explained, pointing out a group of Moslems drinking Turkish coffee in one corner, a number of Buddhists gathered under a Bo-tree, and a group of Catholic nuns striding by, habits flapping in the celestial breeze.

A high wall on one side couldn't obscure the tinkle of piano music, the chink of ice in highball glasses, and the ripple of polite conversation. "And who's behind the wall?" inquired Forman curiously.

"Ssssh," cautioned Angel Gabriel. "Those are the Protestants—and they like to think they're the only ones here."

•

"On my side of the family, we can trace our lineage back to the Tudor kings," Thurston boasted to Howell in the steam room after a grueling game of squash.

"No kidding?" said Howell drily. "And I suppose your folks were right there on the bow of the *Mayflower* too?"

"Of course not," sniffed Thurston. "We always had our own boats."

•

Young Mrs. Townsend wanted very much to participate in the correct charities, and when the annual Junior

League Easter Charity Ball came around, she volunteered to head the committee. It took a lot of organizing, but the party went off without a hitch, and she dined and danced into the wee hours.

When the festivities ended, she was dismayed to observe a bag lady bundled on the sidewalk next to her Saab Turbo. Hearing the rustle of Mrs. Townsend's taffeta skirts, the old woman extended a grimy palm and asked the socialite if she could spare any change.

"Oooh," gasped Mrs. Townsend, "the nerve, and after I spend all night slaving to help people like you! Aren't you ever satisfied?"

•

WASP girl: "How dare you kiss me like that?!"
WASP boy: "Sorry—it was just a slip of the tongue."

•

The Driscolls were driving home from the Forbes' cocktail party when Mindy broke the stony silence. "Why on earth did you tell Chip you married me because I was such a terrific cook? You know I can't boil water, for God's sake."

"Because I had to say *something,*" he retorted.

•

After a very sheltered childhood, it was mildly surprising that Hackley managed to get a decent job, persuade a nice girl to marry him, and father a son and heir. "Now darling," coached his wife, "don't forget to drop by St. Thomas's and ask the Rector to arrange for little Hackley's christening."

"Are you sure about that?" the proud father asked, looking down at the tiny squalling bundle. "He seems awfully small to have a bottle smashed over his head."

•

Orlofski fell in love with the aloof WASP coed at a Mt. Holyoke mixer and married her the day after graduation. It didn't take him long to realize sadly that her reserve carried over into the bedroom as well, despite the new husband's most passionate ministrations. But one night the bedsprings creaked with unusual vigor, and for considerably more than a minute and a half, and Virginia was even heard to utter a small moan. When it was over, she sighed, "I'm just not myself tonight."

"Well," blurted Orlofski, "whoever you were was certainly an improvement."

•

Definition of a WASP:

Someone who thinks Taco Belle is the Mexican phone company.

•

Yuppies don't cry—they just Saab.

•

During brunch at the yacht club, R. Chip Frothingham III took the family doctor aside and confided that he and his wife were having difficulty conceiving.

"I'm not a fertility expert, Chip, but maybe I can help," Dr. Gorham offered kindly. "What position are you in when you ejaculate?"

"Uh . . . what do you mean by ejaculation, Doctor?"

"When you climax?"

The young man still looked blank, so the doctor tried again. "When you come, Chip. Don't you come?"

Chip's face suddenly brightened. "Oh, do you mean that sticky white stuff, Dr. Gorham? Buffy thinks it's yucky, so I make sure to shoot it into the sink before getting into bed."

HANDICAPPED

What song did the mermaid sing to the sailors?

"I can't give you anything but head, baby."

•

The armless man was just starting in on his main course when he realized he had to take a crap, so he summoned the waiter with a nod and asked him to accompany him to the men's room. "Open the stall door, if you'd be so kind," he instructed crisply, "pull my pants down, and close the door. I'll call you when I'm done."

A few moments later the voice of the armless man came over the door of the stall. "Did you hear a splash?"

"No," replied the waiter.

"Goddam it! You forgot to pull down my underwear."

•

The psychiatrist paid close attention as his new client described the situation that was causing him so much anxiety. Afterwards, the psychiatrist confidently told him that it really didn't seem to be a terribly incapacitating problem. "Frankly, Mr. Bach," he said reassuringly, I've known many, many men who prefer boxer shorts to Jockey-type briefs. In fact, I'm one of them."

"Is that so?" A smile came over Bach's face as he leaned over for details. "And do you like them with French dressing or Thousand Island?"

•

Two midgets struck up an acquaintance, and when Hector decided to spend his vacation at a nudist camp in Florida, Martin was extremely curious. He called Hector up the night of his return. "So, how'd it go, what was it like?"

"Frankly, it was a little disconcerting. At first I thought I'd been hijacked to Havana," admitted Hector, "since from my vantage point everybody looked like Fidel Castro."

•

The middle-aged man walked into the bar with a shit-eating grin on his face and ordered a round for the house. "It's nice to see someone in such a good mood," commented the bartender. "Mind if I ask why?"

"This is the happiest day of my life—I'm finally taller than my brother Jim," explained the fellow, beaming from ear to ear.

The bartender studied his customer disbelievingly. "Are you trying to tell me that at your age you actually grew taller?"

"Of course not! See, Jim was in an accident on the Interstate yesterday," he explained cheerfully, "and they had to amputate both his legs."

•

"Mommy, Mommy, I want to go out and play baseball."

"You know you'll scratch the bat with your hooks."

•

"Mommy, Mommy, why can't I go out and play in the snow?"

"You know your iron lung will rust."

•

"Mom, Dad's been run over in the street!"

"Don't make me laugh, Irving. You know my lips are chapped."

•

"Irving, did you get the name of the woman who pushed your wheelchair into a tree?

"No, but I'd recognize that laugh anywhere."

•

"Andrew, I'm really worried about Patty," confessed James to his best friend over the phone. "She wasn't home when I got here, she hasn't called, and it's after midnight. You know how depressed she's been since her mastectomy. Think something could have happened to her?"

"Now try not to worry," soothed his buddy. "Maybe Patty went out for a drink. Maybe she's visiting a friend, know what I mean?"

James glanced at the bedside table and shook his head glumly. "I doubt it. She left her tits behind."

•

How did the sympathetic doctor treat the kleptomaniac?
He gave her something to take.

•

Did you hear about Helen Keller's speech impediment?
Calluses.

•

How come Helen Keller never changed her baby?
So she always knew where to find him.

•

Why did the bike Helen Keller's parents gave her for Christmas come without a front wheel?
So she could feel the road.

•

But what was the meanest present under the Keller Christmas tree?
Rubik's Cube.

•

Okay, but what was the second meanest?
A paint-by-number set.

•

And what was the meanest present Helen Keller ever gave away?
Her first paint-by-number picture.

•

How did the speech therapist strengthen Helen Keller's voice?
He made her practice with a hand squeezer.

•

What was Helen Keller's idea of oral sex?
A manicure.

•

The man came into the psychiatrist's office, reclined on the couch, and told the doctor he needed help ridding his mind of an obsession. "All I can think of, day and night, is making love to a horse. It's driving me nuts."

"I see," said the shrink, rubbing his goatee. "Now would that be to a stallion or to a mare?"

"A mare, of course," retorted the patient, pulling himself upright indignantly. "What do you think I am, a pervert or something?"

•

"What a mob scene," gasped Irene to a woman in her office, as the building lobby grew more and more crowded. "Any idea what's going on, Liz?"

"It's one of those religious maniacs. He's gotten into the center elevator and he's threatening to set himself on fire if anyone approaches him. In fact I figured it might speed things along if I started a collection for him. Feel like donating?"

"Sure, why not. What've you got so far?" asked Irene good-naturedly.

"Seven books of matches and three lighters."

•

How do you circumcise a leper?
Shake him.

•

Mrs. Stone despaired of her humpbacked daughter's marital prospects, since several social seasons in Shaker Heights hadn't produced a single possibility. So she packed her off to Paris, where she hoped the family's considerable fortune would render Jill more attractive.

Sure enough, the girl soon made the acquaintance of a Frenchman from a noble if impoverished family, and when he proposed marriage, she was beside herself with joy. After the final fitting of her Dior wedding dress, Henri took Jill to meet his aged mother, whose consent was necessary. "Don't worry, *ma chèrie,*" he said sweetly, "your refined ways and quaint accent will positively charm Maman. Just one thing, though: you've got to straighten up."

•

Wong hadn't been out of the asylum for long, so his grip on reality was still a little tenuous. And one day as he was walking along, he became obsessed with the need to know the sum of two plus two. Luckily he spotted a psychiatrist's shingle in the next block. The doctor ushered him right in and onto his couch, listened to the question, and informed him gravely that the answer could certainly be worked out after less than a year of biweekly sessions.

Wong rushed out and into the office of an engineer that

happened to be next door. "Two plus two, eh?" muttered the engineer, and began furiously punching numbers into his calculator and adding machine and scribbling on various scraps of paper. Finally he announced that the answer was 3.99999—though he could round it to four if Wong wanted him to.

This still didn't feel right to Wong, who went on until he came to a lawyer's office. He was shown into a book-lined office where the lawyer listened gravely to his question. Then she leaned forward with a warm smile and asked compassionately, "Mr. Wong, tell me—what would you like it to be?"

•

"Note the deformation of the joints due to rheumatic arthritis," lectured the medical school professor, waving his pointer at the illuminated X ray. "In addition, this patient limps because of damage to the right tibia—note the pronounced curvature—sustained in an industrial accident." Turning to the roomful of aspiring radiologists, the professor asked, "Now tell me, in a case like this, what would you do?"

Johannsen stuck up his hand. "Well, sir," he offered, "I bet I'd limp too."

•

When Robinson stretched out on the psychiatrist's couch, he was clearly in a bad state. "Doctor," he pleaded, voice quavering and hands twitching, "you've got to help me. I really think I'm losing my mind. I have no memory of what happened to me a year ago, nor even of a few weeks back. I can't even recall yesterday with any clarity. I can't cope with daily life—in fact, I think I'm going insane."

"Keep calm, Mr. Robinson," soothed the shrink. "I'm sure I'll be able to help you. Now tell me: how long have you had this problem?"

Robinson looked up blankly. "What problem?"

•

"Shep's a really nice guy, Barbara, and I'm sure you really love him, but how can you bear being married to a quadriplegic?" Cynthia marveled to her model girlfriend. "He can't even wiggle his little finger. And let's face it: with your face and your body, you could have picked just about any guy on the planet."

"You don't get it, Cyn," replied Barbara. "Who needs fingers? Shep's tongue is eight inches long."

"An eight-inch tongue?" Cynthia gasped.

"And that's not all," continued Barbara smugly. "He's learned to breathe through his ears."

•

Aunt Jean was rattling along in her Oldsmobile when she got a flat tire. Being an independent sort, she jacked up the car and undid the nuts and bolts, but as she was pulling the tire off, she lost her balance and fell backward onto the hubcap holding the hardware. And it rolled right down into a storm sewer.

This entire incident occurred right outside the state

insane asylum and happened to be observed by an inmate watching carefully through the bars. "Listen, lady," he called out, "just use one bolt from each of the other three tires. They'll be plenty strong enough to get you to the gas station."

"Quick thinking," said Aunt Jean admiringly. "Now why on earth is a bright boy like you stuck in that place?"

"Lady, I'm here for being crazy, not stupid."

CELEBRITIES

What's Billy Martin doing now?
Managing the Angels.

•

Hear how they buried Martin's casket?
All the umpires kicked dirt over it.

•

What were Martin's last words?
"I said 'Bud Light,' not 'Hard right.' "

•

Did you hear that Bush sent Quayle to the epicenter of the San Francisco earthquake?

He cabled back, "Having a great time at Disney World."

•

Did you hear the big new hit in San Francisco?

"Do You Know Another Way to San Jose?"

•

What did Dan Quayle say when he heard about the Berlin Wall?

"Now when are those Chinese going to take down *their* wall?"

•

What's the latest fashion trend in Beijing?

Tank tops.

•

What's the worst thing about massacring a thousand Chinese students?

An hour later, you feel like massacring a thousand more.

•

Jesse Jackson went to the top of the world's highest mountain to discuss the presidential office with God. "Do you think there will ever be a woman President of the U.S.A.?" Jackson asked.

"Not in your lifetime, Jesse," God intoned.

"How about a Jew?" queried the presidential hopeful.

Again God answered, "Not in your lifetime, Jesse."

Finally Jesse asked if there would ever be a black President. And God said, "Not in *my* lifetime, Jesse."

•

What do Mike Dukakis and pantyhose have in common?

They both irritate the bush.

•

What do Dukakis and Alf have in common?

They both like to eat Kitty.

•

Where do watermelons send their kids in the summertime?

To John Cougar Meloncamp.

(See—it wasn't an ethnic joke after all!)

•

Dolly Parton and Princess Di happened to die on the same day and arrive together at the Pearly Gates. "Hello, ladies," St. Peter greeted them. With an apologetic smile, he confessed to a small logistical problem. "I'm afraid we only have room for one person at the moment. And in order to choose between you, I'll have to see what each of you, uh, has to offer."

With a knowing smile, Dolly Parton unbuttoned her blouse, and St. Peter's eyes bulged at the sight of her enormous breasts. Finally tearing his eyes away, he turned to Princess Di, who promptly hiked up her skirt and proceeded to give herself a douche. As soon as she was finished, the saint took her by the elbow and started to lead her into Heaven.

"Now wait just a minute, Pete," protested Dolly. "What was so special about that?"

"Aw, honey," explained St. Peter, turning back with a shrug, "you know a royal flush beats a pair any time."

•

What's black and crisp and comes on a stick?

Joan of Arc.

•

How come they took John Wayne Toilet Paper off the market?

Because it was rough and tough and didn't take shit off of anyone.

•

What's blue and red and spins around and around?
A Smurf in a blender.

•

What's red, soft, wiggles, shimmies and shakes?
The Blob having an orgasm.

•

When Buckwheat grew up and changed his name, what did he decide to call himself?
Kareem of Wheat!

•

Did you know that an Italian actor was going to star in *Beverly Hills Cop* before Eddie Murphy got the part?
It was going to be called *Beverly Hills Wop.*

•

Did you hear about poor Roman Polanski's latest tragedy?
His new wife just passed away—crib death.

•

What's the difference between a moose and Guy Lombardo's orchestra?

With a moose the horns are in the front and the asshole's in the rear.

•

When Reagan died and went to Hell, he was given the customary tour, past the cauldrons of boiling oil, the bottomless pits, the hapless souls chained amidst searing flames. Eventually he passed a cesspool full to the brim with unthinkable slime and filth, and who should be occupying it but the old Watergate gang. John Dean was standing waist-deep in the foul muck, Haldeman and Ehrlichman were up to their necks, and next to them was a knee-deep John Mitchell.

"Hey," asked Reagan, holding his nose and turning to the Devil, "how come Mitchell's gotten off so lightly?"

"It's all relative," the Devil explained. "He's balancing on Nixon's shoulders."

•

Did you hear that Mel Brooks is putting together a new movie, starring Michael Jackson and Richard Pryor?

It's going to be called *Blazing Sambos*!

•

When the brash young advertising executive arrived at La Coupole for his lunch appointment, he spotted Donald Trump at a corner table and went right over. "Excuse me for interrupting your meal, Mr. Trump," he began, "but I know how much you appreciate enterprise and initiative. I'm trying to win over a very important account today—it could really make or break my company—and the clients I'm meeting with would be incredibly impressed if you stopped by our table at some point and said, 'Hello, Mike.' It would be an incredible favor, Mr. Trump, and someday I'd make it up to you."

"Okay, okay," sighed Trump, and went back to his smoked pheasant. He finished and was putting on his coat when he remembered the young man's request. Obligingly he went over to his table, tapped him on the shoulder, and said, "Hi, Mike."

"Not now, Donald," interrupted the young man. "Can't you see I'm eating?"

•

What's blonde, has big boobs, and lives in Sweden?

Salman Rushdie.

•

What's the difference between Elvis and Salman Rushdie?

Elvis lives.

•

Margaret Thatcher and her Cabinet were meeting over lunch to discuss an important bit of impending legislation. "And what will you have, Madam?" asked the waiter, coming over with his note pad.

"I'll have the Beef Wellington," replied the Prime Minister promptly, eager to get on with the business at hand.

"And for the vegetables?" continued the waiter politely.

Thatcher replied briskly, "They'll have the same."

•

The attractive woman turned to the man in the business suit behind her in the elevator. "Excuse me," she asked, "but are you Donald Trump?"

The man cleared his throat. "Yes, as a matter of fact, I am."

"Oh," she gushed, "I've *always* wanted to meet you, Mr. Trump. And now that we're together," she continued throatily, "I'll tell you what I'd like to do: I'm inviting you back to my room, where I'll kneel in front of you and pull out your cock and suck it till you have a giant hard-on and suck it some more until you come all over my face . . ."

"I don't know," said Trump, thinking it over. "What's in it for me?"

MALE ANATOMY

Mort knew he was probably oversensitive about the problem, but the fact was that his eyes bulged out. He went to doctor after doctor, but none seemed to know of any treatment, and in desperation he looked up "Eyes Bulging Out" in the Yellow Pages. Sure enough a doctor was listed, and a few days later Mort found himself sitting on a vinyl couch in a seedy waiting room. A little nervous about being the only patient, he reminded himself how rare the condition was and that the doctor *was* a specialist.

At long last he was admitted to the doctor's office and examined. The doctor leaned back and informed him that there was a remedy, but not an easy one. "I must cut your balls off," he said.

Mort's eyes bulged out even more as he headed for the door. But after a few weeks of thinking it over, Mort acknowledged that his bulging eyes were what kept him from getting laid in the first place, so he decided to go ahead with the operation. He returned for the operation, and sure enough, his eyeballs sank back into their sockets most agreeably. In fact, he looked not only normal but actually rather handsome.

Delighted, he thanked the doctor profusely, and decided to treat his remodeled self to a new suit. "Charcoal grey pinstripe," he instructed the tailor. "Medium lapel, no cuffs."

"Fine," said the tailor, nodding. "Come back on Tuesday."

"Aren't you going to measure me?" asked Mort.

"Nah. I've been at this over thirty years. I can tell your size just by looking," the tailor assured him.

"That's impossible," blurted Mort.

"Size forty-two jacket, right?"

"Yes," admitted Mort, amazed.

"Thirty-two-inch inseam, right?"

Mort nodded, dumbstruck.

"Thirty-six-inch waist?"

Again Mort nodded.

"And you wear size forty underwear, right?" concluded the tailor with a smile.

"Nope!" Mort told him. "Thirty-four."

"Listen, you can't fool me," said the tailor wearily. "Don't even try to put one over."

"I'm telling you, I wear size thirty-four underwear," Mort insisted.

"You *can't* wear size thirty-four underwear," protested the exasperated tailor. "Your eyes would bulge out of their sockets!"

•

Joe and Moe went outside to take a leak and Joe confessed, "I wish I had one like my cousin Junior. He needs four fingers to hold his."

Moe looked over and pointed out, "But you're holding *yours* with four fingers."

"I know," said Joe with a sigh, "but I'm peeing on three of them."

•

What would you call a comedian whose underwear was too tight?

Dickie Smothers.

•

Bert had just turned fifty and became concerned that his stamina in bed was really declining. So he went to consult his doctor, who pointed out that his general physical condition left something to be desired. "You're a little overweight, you're easily winded, you're just out of shape. I recommend jogging five miles a day," said the doctor. "It'll really improve your stamina in general." And though Bert was a couch potato by nature, he reluctantly agreed to the regimen.

A week later, the phone rang. "Hi Bert, how're you feeling?" asked the doctor.

"Really terrific," enthused his patient.

"And how's your sex life?"

"What sex life?" countered Bert. "I'm thirty-five miles from home."

•

Why's it so easy to turn on Frankenstein's monster?

Because he has amps in his pants.

•

When the doctor pulled down Johnson's pants, he was shocked to discover that his penis was a mangled wreck. "Jesus!" he couldn't help exclaiming. "What the hell happened to you?"

Despite his pain, Johnson blushed. "I had a real good thing going, Doc," he explained. "See, the girl who lives next to me in the trailer park was widowed not too long ago. When she gets lonely, she takes a knothole out of the floor, puts in a hot dog, and goes to work squatting over it. So I figured to myself, why not get in on the action?" A dreamy look came over Johnson's face.

"And then?" prodded the doctor.

"Everything was going great until last night," said Johnson, wincing. "Some son of a bitch rang the doorbell and she tried to kick the hot dog under the stove."

•

When the traveling salesman got the message at the hotel desk that his wife had given birth, he rushed to the phone. "Hi honey," he cried happily. "Is it a boy or a girl?"

"Irving, Irving," sighed his wife wearily, "is that all you can think about? Sex, sex, sex?"

•

Philip and Michael were live-in lovers. One day Philip called in sick, and Michael called home in the middle of the morning to see how he was feeling. "Oh, by the way," he asked, "did the paper boy come yet?"

"No," answered Michael, "but he's got that glassy look in his eye. . . ."

•

Ohrenstein was less than pleased with the doctor's remedy for the constant fatigue that was plaguing him. "Give up sex completely, Doctor?" he screamed. "I'm a young guy. How can you expect me to just go cold turkey?"

"So get married and taper off gradually," advised the physician.

•

When O'Connor went in for his physical, he confessed that his sexual performance wasn't all it could be. "Haven't you got any medication that could help me out?"

The doctor hemmed and hawed, but finally pulled out a vial of small blue pills. "These should do the trick," he told his patient, dismissing him.

"Boy, you weren't kidding," yelled O'Connor into the phone a few hours later. "Three times already!"

"Fine, fine," nodded the doctor, smiling. "And your wife, is she pleased?"

"I don't know," said the grateful patient. "She's not home from work yet."

•

When Ernie walked into the pharmacy and asked for rubbers, the girl behind the counter asked politely, "What size, please?"

"Gee, I don't know," answered Ernie, a little flustered, so she instructed him to use the fence out back to determine the correct size. And as he walked out the back door, she ran out a side door and behind the fence.

The fence had three holes in it.

Putting his penis in the first hole, Ernie felt capable hands gently stroking it. Reluctantly, he pulled it out and inserted it in the second hole, and within seconds, he felt a warm, wet pussy at work on the other side of the fence. Groaning with pleasure, he managed to pull out and stick it through the third hole. There he felt an expert set of lips and tongue give him the blow job of his dreams. Jumping up, the salesgirl hurried back behind the counter and was standing there smiling when Ernie staggered back through the door.

"Your size, sir?" she asked politely.

"Forget the rubbers," he grunted. "Just gimme three yards of that fence."

•

After the birth of his third child, Warner decided to have a vasectomy. During the operation, one of his testicles accidentally fell on the floor, and before the nurse could scoop it back up, the doctor had stepped on it. Unfazed, the doctor simply asked the nurse for a small onion, which he proceeded to suture inside the scrotum.

Two weeks later Warner was back for his post-op checkup. "How's it going?" asked the doctor.

"I gotta tell you, I'm having some problems," admitted the patient.

"Such as?"

"Well, Doc, every time I take a leak, my eyes water; every time I come, I get heartburn; and every time I pass a Burger King, I get a hard-on!"

•

A woodpecker from North Carolina flew up to the Catskills for his summer vacation. He went to work on his first lodgepole pine, *rat-tat-tat-tat-tat,* when a bolt of lightning struck the tree and split it right down the middle.

"God *damn* it," grumbled the woodpecker. "It never fails to astound me how hard my pecker gets when I'm away from home."

•

Terribly agitated, Jack rushed into his dentist's examining room and ushered the hygienist firmly to the door. Once he was alone with the doctor, he unzipped his fly and gingerly pulled out his dick.

"Jack, Jack," said the dentist, taken aback. "I'm a dentist. If you think you have V.D., you need to see your regular doctor."

"It's not V.D." gasped Jack, "and you've gotta help me. There's a tooth embedded in it."

•

Jose cracked up when he came home and found his wife ironing her brassiere. "Why bother?" he asked, wiping tears of laughter off his cheeks. "You got nothing to put in it."

"Is that so?" she shot back. "I iron your shorts, don't I?"

•

Bill was pretty naive when it came to sex, so he decided to take matters into his own hands and pay a visit to the local prostitute. But no sooner had he been shown into her room and taken down his pants, than he shot his wad.

"Too bad, sonny," commiserated the hooker. "Can you come again?"

"Oh, no problem," Bill replied cheerfully. "I live right in the neighborhood."

•

Casey made an appointment with a sex therapist and explained that he and his wife were unable to achieve simultaneous climax. "It's not a terrible problem, Doctor," he conceded, "but isn't there something I could do about it?"

The therapist confided that he and his wife had had the same problem, which he'd solved by hiding a pistol under his pillow. "When I was about to come, I reached for the gun and fired a shot, and Doreen climaxed with me. Come back next week and tell me how it works for you."

That very night the therapist got a call from the county hospital and rushed over to the emergency room. "What happened, Casey?" he cried, catching sight of his patient writhing in pain on an examining table, clutching a bloodsoaked towel to his groin.

Wincing, Casey explained that he'd gone right out to purchase a .45, hid it under the pillow, and started making love to his wife. "And when I was about to come, I grabbed the gun and fired."

"So?" pursued the doctor.

"She shat in my face and bit off the end of my dick."

•

What does a man have in his pants that a woman doesn't want on her face?

Wrinkles!

FEMALE ANATOMY

When the gynecologist confirmed her suspicion that she was pregnant, Celeste got a little scared. "It'll be my first baby," she confessed with a blush, "and actually I don't know the first thing about how babies are delivered."

"Don't worry about a thing," reassured the doctor. "It's really not all that different from how the baby got started in the first place."

Startled, Celeste exclaimed, "You mean twice around the park with my legs hanging out of the cab?"

•

What's the first thing a sorority girl does in the morning?

Goes home.

•

The god of thunder and lightning banged on the door of the local prostitute's house, demanding entry. "I am mighty Thor," he roared.

The weary prostitute opened the door a crack and replied, "Tho am I, buddy, tho am I."

•

Why do Canadian women use hockey pucks instead of tampons?

Because they last for three periods.

•

The dentist was called away from the dinner table to take an urgent phone call. It was Mr. Tuckerman, explaining that young Junior had gotten himself into quite a fix. "See, he was kissing his girlfriend Corinne, and when my wife and I came back from the movies we found them stuck together."

"I'll come right over, Mr. Tuckerman," said the dentist calmly, "and don't worry about a thing. I have to unlock teenagers' braces all the time."

"Yes, but from an IUD?"

•

Bumper sticker:

If girls are all sugar and spice . . .
Why do they taste like anchovies?

•

When Jackie went to the dentist for the first time in years, she was prepared for bad news. Nevertheless she was a little put out when, after some time, the dentist gasped, "Jesus, what happened to your teeth? They're all gone, and your gums are in terrible shape?"

"If it's such a big problem," Jackie retorted, "then get your face out of my lap."

•

What do you get when you cross a hooker with a pit bull?

The last blow job you'll ever get.

•

What's hairy and conquered Asia?

Genghis Cunt.

•

Orville went to specialist after specialist in search of a diagnosis, and it finally emerged that he was suffering from a rare enzymatic disorder, the only treatment for which was fresh breast milk. So he advertised in the want ads for a wet nurse, and was delighted when a woman promptly responded. Explaining the situation over the phone, he negotiated a fee and made an appointment for the next day.

It so happened that Orville had always been a tit man and had an exceptionally skilled set of lips and tongue, and that after a few minutes the woman found herself extremely aroused.

Squirming, breathing heavily, she managed to gasp, "Uh . . . is there anything else I could offer you?"

"Mmm," murmured Orville, looking up and wiping his chin. "You don't happen to have any Oreos, do you?"

•

Hear about the gynecologist who started going to an analyst . . .

. . . because he was always feeling low?

•

What do you call an anorexic with a yeast infection?

A quarter-pounder with cheese.

•

The obese woman made an appointment for a physical examination, after which she was summoned into the doctor's office. "You're in very good health, Mrs. Bloom," he said, his nose wrinkling in distaste. "But I must speak frankly: in my many years of practice, I have never come across a patient whose personal hygiene was worse than yours. In fact, without a doubt you are the most disgusting, revolting, physically repellent creature ever to have crossed my path in my entire life."

"Hmmmm," mused Mrs. Bloom. "You know, Doctor, a gynecologist told me exactly the same thing last week."

"Then why on earth did you consult me?" he asked.

"Oh, you know how it is, Doctor," she explained. "I just wanted a second opinion."

•

Have you heard the nightgown song?

"Love Lifted Me."

•

Mike was touching up the paint in the bathroom one weekend when the brush slipped out of his hand, leaving a stripe across the toilet seat. So Mike painted the whole seat over, and went off to a ball game.

His wife happened to get home early, went upstairs to pee, and found herself firmly stuck to the toilet seat. At six o'clock Mike found her there, furious and embarrassed, but was unable to dislodge her for fear of tearing the skin.

With considerable difficulty Mike managed to get her into the back seat of the car and then into a wheelchair at the county hospital, where she was wheeled into a room and maneuvered, on her knees, onto an examining table. At this point the resident entered and surveyed the scene. "What do you think, Doc?" broke in the nervous husband.

"Nice, very nice," he commented, stroking his chin. "But why the cheap frame?"

•

How do you qualify to be the girlfriend of a Hell's Angel?
You have to be able to suck start a Harley.

•

Doctor: Mr. Franklin, I asked you to come by today so that we could discuss your wife's condition.
Franklin: Certainly, Doctor.
Doctor: It appears, Mr. Franklin, that your wife has acute angina.
Franklin: I couldn't agree more . . . but what's wrong with her?

•

What's hairy and sucks blood?
Cunt Dracula.

•

Arlene got on the phone to her lawyer and declared, "I want a divorce."

"Jeez, this is kind of sudden," the lawyer commented. "Do you have grounds?"

"Sure do—the apartment in the city and a beach house on Fire Island."

The lawyer persisted. "What I mean is, do you have some kind of grudge?"

"Not exactly, but there's parking underneath the building," Arlene replied brightly.

"That's not what I mean," he said, growing exasperated. "Your husband Joe, does he beat you up or something?"

"Oh, no, I'm the first one up every morning."

"Arlene!" yelled the lawyer. "Can you just tell me why you want a divorce?"

"Certainly: it's because I just can't carry on a decent conversation with the man."

•

Why are most hookers immune to men?

Because they've been inoculated so many times.

•

Did you hear the one about the lady who got pregnant while she was working at the sperm bank?

She was arrested for embezzlement.

•

A certain young lady from Wheeling
Claimed to lack all sexual feeling
Till a cynic named Boris
Merely touched her clitoris
And she had to be scraped off the ceiling.

•

Shatzkin was used to the occasional late-night call, usually from a client who'd had an accident of some sort, but on this night it was an agitated woman obviously in the middle of a violent argument with her husband.

"Tell me, Mr. Shatzkin," she yelled over the noise of her mate's ranting in the background, "if a husband leaves his wife, is she or is she not legally entitled to the house and its contents?"

"I can't give such advice over the phone, especially without knowing the particulars of the case," the lawyer reasonably pointed out. "Call my office in the morning and we'll set up an appointment."

The background roars had subsided, and the woman continued in a normal tone without skipping a beat. "She's also entitled to the time-share, both cars, and the joint savings account? Thank you very much," she said in a triumphant tone, and hung up.

•

Did you hear about the girl who had tits on her back?

She was ugly to look at, but a whole lot of fun to dance with.

•

What did the prostitute say to the long-forgotten friend?

"Bend over—I think I know you."

•

The fellow made an appointment with the town banker and explained with great excitement that he'd come across a formula which would make pussy smell like an orange. "All I need's a little cash to start up with."

The banker listened politely but turned down the loan, remarking that it just didn't sound to him like a sound business proposition. A year or so later, though, he noticed that the man's bank account had swelled to impressive proportions, so the banker invited him back for a second meeting. "Say, I hope there are no hard feelings about my turning down that loan last year," he said bluntly.

"Nope, none at all," replied the entrepreneur cheerfully. "In fact, quite the opposite. See, you got me to thinking, and I figured you had a point. So I went to work on a formula to make an orange taste like pussy—and it's selling like crazy."

HOMOSEXUAL

Why do so few gays play the flute?
They're always forgetting to blow instead of suck.

•

What's another name for AIDS?
Goner-rhea.

•

What's Preparation H?
Dingleberry jam.

•

What did the lesbian gas station attendant say when the leggy blonde pulled in?
"Mind if I check under your hood?"

•

"Mommy, one of the kids at school called me a sissy."

"So what did you do, Benny?"

"I hit him with my purse."

•

Chad was thrilled to run into Bart on Christopher Street and gave him a big hug. "Sweetie, I've been so worried about you," he cried. "I thought you were doing time on that nasty sodomy charge."

Bart grinned. "I got myself a smart lawyer who got the charge reduced to 'following too closely.' "

•

If you get malaria from mosquitoes and Lyme disease from ticks, what do you get AIDS from?

Asshoppers.

•

Two homosexuals were out driving one weekend, and when Jerry's hand slipped between Kevin's thighs, Kevin got distracted and ran right into the truck double-parked in the right lane.

"You blind idiot," bellowed the burly truck driver, jumping out of the cab and stalking over in a rage. He escalated into a string of epithets and obscenities, finally leaning into the window and screaming, "And you can kiss my ass!" in Kevin's ear.

"Now you stop that talk," admonished the fag, who until then had remained silent through the whole tirade. "This is no time to make love."

•

What do you call a gay fruit?

A figgit.

•

And what's the queerest type of bread?

Humpernickel.

•

Delbert was window shopping in some of New York's sexual-paraphernalia stores. When he spotted a particularly realistic black rubber phallus, the fag went inside. "I'll take that one," he told the clerk, pointing at the object of his desire.

"Fine, buddy. You need it wrapped?"

"Don't bother," replied Delbert. "I'll eat it right here."

•

Why are male prostitutes like Inspector Clousseau?
They're both Peter Sellers.

•

What's a gay masochist?
A sucker for punishment.

•

Handsome Vinnie had a great vacation visiting the backroom of every gay bar on Castro Street, but it left him somewhat the worse for wear. When he got home he called up a friend who practiced homeopathic medicine and complained that his rectum was terribly swollen and tender. The friend recommended making a poultice of herbal tea leaves and applying it to the area.

It did relieve the irritation a bit, but the next morning found Vinnie still in considerable discomfort, so he hobbled over to the office of a proctologist who served the gay community. In the examining room, the good-looking fellow bent over and spread his cheeks. The doctor clucked sympathetically and started investigating.

"Well, Doctor?" asked Vinnie after a few minutes had passed. "What's the diagnosis?"

"It's not completely clear, darling," admitted the proctologist, "but the tea leaves recommend a Caribbean cruise for the two of us."

•

What's another name for a sex-change operation?
Artificial infemination.

•

Late one night three masked men stormed into a night club in Greenwich Village. Brandishing pistols, they ordered everyone onto the floor. "Now we're going to rape all the men and rob all the broads," leered one big fellow.

"No, no, no," interrupted the other. "We rape the women and rob the men."

"Say, I think you should listen to that first fellow," piped up a fag in the corner.

•

Why is there no law against masturbation?
People would take it into their own hands.

•

Did you hear about the transvestite who had two breasts grafted onto his back?
If his ass holds out, he'll be a millionaire.

•

Beset with grief, a poor homosexual had just found out that he had AIDS. "What am I going to do?" pleaded the man after his doctor had reviewed the prognosis.

"I think you should go to Mexico and live it up. Drink

the water and eat all the Mexican cuisine you can get your hands on, including raw fruits and vegetables," advised the doctor.

"Oh, God, Doc, will that cure me?" squealed the gay.

"No," answered the doctor candidly, "but it'll teach you what your asshole is for."

RELIGIOUS

Three aged nuns decided to take a well-deserved vacation in Bermuda. None had ever been out of Massachusetts before, so their first night they compared notes on the marvels of the tropics. "The size of the grapefruits," gasped Sister Mary Joseph, hands circling the air expressively.

"And the bananas," added Sister Ignatius, also gesturing appropriately.

"Eh?" chipped in Sister Jean-Baptiste, who was hard of hearing. "Father who?"

•

What's the special at fast-food restaurants for cannibals?

An all-beef missionary, special sauce, lettuce, cheese and onions, on a sesame-seed bun.

•

The very distinguished bishop and the terribly eminent judge were both asked to deliver speeches at their thirtieth college reunion. Afterwards they met up at the buffet, and engaged in a little banter over which of them had more influence over the common man. "Let's face it, old boy," said the bishop rather condescendingly, "in your courtroom, the worst thing you can say is 'You be hanged!' While I ultimately have far more power: to the same fellow I can declare, 'You be damned!' "

"True," conceded the judge with a smile, "but there's a crucial difference. When I say to a man, 'You be hanged!' —he *is* hanged!"

•

The penniless teacher watched in desperation as his beloved wife was seized by some sort of wasting disease and grew weaker each day. Finally he called the only doctor in the whole district and begged him to treat his wife. "I'll give you everything I own," he begged. "Just come."

"She sounds very ill," the doctor pointed out. "What if I'm unable to cure her?"

"I'll pay, I'll pay," swore the teacher. "Just get here as soon as possible."

So the doctor paid a call, but nevertheless the patient died a few days later. And soon afterward the doctor's considerable bill arrived. The distraught teacher realized he couldn't possibly pay it, so he called upon the rabbi to arbitrate the case. Asked for his side of the story, the irritated doctor said firmly, "This man promised to pay me whether the patient lived or died."

"Did you cure her?" asked the rabbi thoughtfully.

"No," admitted the physician.

"And did you kill her?"

"Absolutely not!" he protested indignantly.

"In that case," the rabbi pronounced firmly, "you have no grounds on which to base a fee."

•

In the middle of the night, Father MacDonagh was dragged out of his hut by a furious mob of aborigines. Before he was even fully awake, he found himself tied to a stubby tree atop a pile of kindling. "Stop!" he shrieked at the aborigine leader, who was approaching with a flaming torch. "I'm your friend. Why are you doing this to me!?!"

An evil leer on his face, the chief explained that a woman in their village had given birth to a mulatto child. "Since no other white man lives within ten days' walk, you must be the father. And you must die."

Sweating profusely and thinking fast, Father MacDonagh beckoned the aborigine over with a wave of his head. "Do you remember the black lamb born to my flock of white ewes last spring?" The chief nodded, and the priest continued sagely, "Well, there aren't any black rams in this territory, are there?" The chief extinguished his torch, looked around, and proposed in a whisper, "I keep your secret, you keep mine."

•

Seated next to an aged rabbi on a transcontinental flight, the eager young priest couldn't resist the opportunity to proselytise. "You really should think about coming over to the Roman Catholic faith, being welcomed into the arms of the Holy Father," he enthused. "It is the only true faith, you know—only those who believe in the Sacraments shall be admitted to the Kingdom of Heaven when they die."

The rabbi nodded indulgently but expressed no interest in the mechanics of conversion, and eventually the young priest fell silent, depressed by his failure. Soon after, the plane ran into a tremendous hurricane, lost power, and crashed into the Illinois countryside. Miraculously the priest was thrown, unhurt, from his seat. When he came to and looked back at the flaming wreckage, the first thing he saw was the rabbi, making the sign of the cross.

Crossing himself and whispering a brief prayer of gratitude, the priest ran over and took his arm. "Praise the Lord!" he babbled joyfully, "You *did* hear the Word after all, didn't you? And just in time for it to comfort you through mortal peril. And you do wish to be saved, to become one of us now. Halleluiah!"

"Vat on earth are you talking about?" asked the elderly fellow, still rather dazed.

"Sir, I saw it with my own eyes. As you stepped out of the flames, you made the sign of the cross!"

"Cross? Vat cross?" asked the rabbi irritably. "I vas simply checking: spectacles, testicles, vallet and vatch."

•

It was necessary for Reverend Addison to engage the services of a lawyer to negotiate a small property dispute. He was quite discomfited to receive a sizeable bill, and decided to drop by the attorney's office to see if the matter could be rectified. "You see," he explained ingratiatingly, "I had been given to understand that members of the bar were not in the habit of charging men of the cloth for their services."

"Allow me to correct you," said the lawyer, unswayed by the minister's righteous demeanor. "You clergymen may look to your reward in the next world, but we lawyers require ours in this one."

•

Ogilvie worked so hard putting himself through school and starting his own company that he had no time to devote to any sort of social or family life. But when he reached his forties and had succeeded in amassing a considerable fortune, he decided it was time to marry—and that only a virgin would be suitable. He realized the odds were against him, so he decided to adopt a baby girl and have her raised in a monastery in rural France until she was of marriageable age.

Fortunately Ogilvie was a patient man, but even so, sixteen years was a long time to wait. By the time a dour nun had escorted the lovely young woman across the Atlantic, the marriage had been performed, and Ogilvie had carried her across the threshold of his magnificent house, he was trembling in anticipation. Gently he laid his delicate bride down on the bed, then reached into a drawer and pulled out a tube of K-Y jelly he'd had the forethought to purchase in advance.

"An' what would that be for?" asked the girl curiously.

"So it won't hurt when I enter you, dearest," he explained tenderly.

She dismissed the tube with a wave. "An' why not just spit on your cock the way the monks did?"

CRUELTY TO ANIMALS

Myron's mother was very hard to please, but one year he thought hard and finally came up with a truly inspired birthday present: a gorgeous parrot that spoke six languages. He paid the exorbitant price and ordered the bird delivered to her apartment in an ornate antique cage on the appointed day.

That evening he came by for the birthday dinner. "So, Mom, did you get my present?" he asked casually.

"Yes, Myron, I did. And I must say it's cooked up very nicely."

"You didn't cook it!" gasped Myron. "Mom, that bird cost me fifteen hundred dollars. And it spoke English, Portuguese, Mandarin, Urdu, Arabic, and Russian!"

"Now, Myron," the old woman chided, "if it really spoke all those languages, why didn't it say something?"

•

Forced by a team of cunning and venal attorneys into a disastrous divorce settlement, Swenson decided to try and forget his woes by taking a vacation out West. Putting distance between himself and his problems didn't help much, though, so Swenson went into the nearest town and started to drown his sorrows in the corner tavern. He fell to mulling over his divorce again, and soon blurted out, "Goddamn lawyers—they're all a bunch of horses' asses."

"For God's sake, Mister," said the bartender, rushing over and addressing Swenson in a stage whisper, "don't say things like that around here. Don't you know you're in horse country?"

•

When Felice's sailor husband was called up on a tour of duty that would have him away for almost a year, she was a little nervous, and sure enough the house was broken into a week after he'd left. So she decided to buy herself a dog for protection.

But the pet-shop owner persuaded her that he had something ten times better than any attack dog. "It's a karate monkey," he explained. "Trained by a black belt and smarter than any dog. Watch this." The shopkeeper turned to the monkey, which looked harmless enough, and ordered, "Karate that chair!" The monkey leapt into action and the chair was reduced to splinters in twenty seconds.

Impressed, Felice bought the little creature, but once she had it home she was beset by doubts again. So she took it out into the backyard and commanded, "Karate that tree!" In less than a minute, the oak was reduced to kindling. Felice was delighted, and the monkey kept her safe and sound until her husband returned from the sea one afternoon, roaring drunk.

"What the hell's that?" he blustered, pointing at the animal.

"It's a karate monkey, dear," she explained, "to protect me."

"Oh yeah?" roared the sailor. "Karate, my ass!"

•

What's the difference between a porcupine and two lawyers in a BMW?

A porcupine has the pricks on the outside.

•

Shirley had always wanted to see Australia, so she saved up her money and went off on a two-week tour. And she'd only been there three days when she fell head over heels in love with a kangaroo. So she blithely disregarded the advice of her tour guide and companions, had an aboriginal priest perform a wedding ceremony, and brought her new husband back to her house in the Midwest.

But she found that the course of true love was not without its problems, and in a few months decided to consult a marriage counselor. "Frankly, in your case it's not hard to put my finger on the heart of the problem," said the counselor almost immediately. "Besides the obvious ethnic and cultural differences between you and your husband, it's clearly going to be impossible to establish genuine lines of communication with a kangaroo."

"Oh, that's not it at all," Shirley broke in. "My husband and I communicate perfectly—except in bed. There it's nothing but hop on, hop off, hop on, hop off. . . ."

•

"I hope you can help me, Dr. Berg," said the woman to a podiatrist. "My feet hurt me all the time."

The doctor asked her to walk down the hall and back while he observed, and when she sat back down he pointed out that she was extremely bowlegged. "Do you know if this is a congenital problem?"

"Oh no, it developed quite recently. You see, I've been screwing doggie fashion a lot."

"Well I'd recommend trying another sexual position," said the doctor, slightly taken aback.

"No way," she replied tartly. "That's the only way my Doberman will fuck."

•

Sherman was the first boy to leave the little town in Louisiana for a fancy Northern university, so as a parting gesture his parents offered him Lil' Jack, their blue tick hound, to keep him company amongst all those Yankees. So Sherman and the dog headed off and settled in fine, until he got a call from Sue Ellen, his hometown girl. It seemed that a little problem was going to materialize in eight months unless Sherman sent her some money to get it taken care of. So Sherman put in a call to the parents.

"Oh, I'm doing fine," he told them, "but Lil' Jack is kind of depressed. See, all these Yankee dogs already know how to read and do geometry, and it's getting him down. But there's a lady here who can teach him all that stuff, and she only charges five hundred dollars."

Sherman's parents agreed that they couldn't let the family dog down, so they sent him the money and he delivered it to Sue Ellen. And everything was fine for two months or so, until Sue Ellen informed him that another expensive problem was on the way.

Sherman got on the phone again. "Oh, I'm doing fine," he assured his parents, "but frankly Lil' Jack's another story. See, he's read all the books in the university library—why, he's subscribed to any number of magazines—but these Yankee dogs can talk as well as you and I do. And as you can imagine, it's gotten him a little depressed. But for only five hundred dollars, that same lady can teach him to talk English, and French to boot."

Maw and Paw again agreed that they couldn't let Lil' Jack down, and wired Sherman the money. And everything was fine until Sherman was driving home for Christmas vacation, Lil' Jack in the back seat, and wondering what the hell he was going to tell his parents. He thought and thought and thought, and when he reached the farm next door to his parents', he took his shotgun, stepped into the ditch, whistled for Lil' Jack, and shot the dog through the head.

"So where's that dadburn dog?" asked Paw, after giving his son a big hug in the driveway.

"It was a hell of a drive, Paw," answered Sherman, "what with Lil' Jack reciting Baudelaire and explaining trigonometry and going on about Shakespeare's tragic vision when we happen to drive past Hickford's farm. And what should Lil' Jack ask me but, 'Sherman, what do you think your Paw would do if I mentioned to Maw how he's been sneaking over and boffing Mrs. Hickford every week or so for five years now?' "

"Sherman," said Paw, gravely taking his son by the shoulders, "you shot that dog, didn't you?"

•

"Now cheer up, Paul," soothed his buddy Bill over a couple of Budweisers. "You and Louise seem to be doing just fine. And it seems a little silly for you to be jealous of a German shepherd, frankly. After all, you work all day and you live out in the sticks. That dog's good company for Louise."

"Good company!" snorted Paul, nearly spilling his beer. "Hey, the other night I caught her douching with Gravy Train."

•

A man was charged with shooting a number of prize quail being raised on a farmer's adjoining piece of woodland. The counsel for the defense opted for an aggressive opening. "Tell me, sir," he challenged, "are you prepared to swear that that man shot your quail?"

"Hold your horses, young man," rejoined the farmer calmly. "I said I *suspected* him of shooting my birds."

"Ah *hah!*" crowed the attorney. "And just why is it that you came to suspect that gentleman in particular?"

"First of all, I heard a gun go off and saw some quail fall out of the sky," retorted the farmer testily. "Second, well onto my property I came across that very fellow with a gun and a bird dog. Third, I found three of my quail in his pocket . . . and I don't reckon they flew in there and committed suicide."

•

A snake had the misfortune to be born blind, and though he managed to forage successfully, he was very lonely. So he was delighted to make the acquaintance of a little mole—which was very nearly blind, as such creatures are—who offered to be his friend.

They got together nearly every day, and finally the snake mustered up his courage to ask the mole a question. "We have become dear friends, and yet I have no idea what you look like," he pointed out. "Would you mind if I coiled myself around you very gently so I could get an image of you?"

"Not at all," replied the mole graciously, and soon found himself in the center of a mountain of snake.

"Why, you are soft and furry, with a pointy little nose surrounded by bristly whiskers. Could it be that you are a mole?" hissed the snake.

"I am indeed," answered the mole. "And you—you are cold and slimy and are covered with scales and have no balls."

"Ssssshit," hissed the snake, "I must be a lawyer."

•

Did you hear about the lion who consulted an eminent Beverly Hills psychiatrist?

The king of the beasts complained that every time he roared, he had to sit through a two-hour movie.

OLD AGE

What's the difference between an old man and a penis?
When you hold a penis, the wrinkles disappear.

•

Judge Wade was considered pretty hard-hearted, but even he was moved by the aging prostitute's tale of hardship and woe. Before handing down a sentence he ordered a recess, and was mulling the case over on the way back to his chambers when he ran into a colleague. "Say," he asked, "what would you give a down-and-out fifty-seven-year-old hooker?"

"Ten bucks, max," replied the other judge.

•

"I just hope it's not Alzheimer's," confessed Lundqvist. "Maybe there's some kind of memory medicine you can give me. See, I'm getting terribly forgetful; I lose track of where I'm going or what I'm supposed to do when I get there. What should I do?" he asked glumly.

"Pay me in advance," the doctor promptly suggested.

•

How can you tell when you're getting old?

When you've been with a woman all night and the only thing that comes is daylight.

•

Harold saved for years and years for his dream vacation —a weekend in Nevada, where prostitution was legal. However, since Harold worked for barely the minimum wage, the years stretched into decades, and so he was ninety-one when he got off the bus in Reno in front of a glitzy bordello.

Harold tottered up to the front desk. "Isn't this Adelaide's famous Pleasure Palace?" he asked.

"Why, yes," replied the incredulous receptionist. "How can I help you?"

"Don't you have the most beautiful gals in town lined up and waiting?" Harold quavered. The receptionist nodded. "Well, I'm here to get laid."

"How old are you, Pops?" she asked bluntly.

"I'm ninety-one."

"Ninety-one! Pops, you've *had* it."

"Oh, really?" A disconcerted look passed over the old man's face as his trembling fingers reached for his wallet. "What do I owe you?"

•

Just as the elderly woman was turning her Mercedes into a parking space at the mall, she was edged out by a red Firebird. "You've got to be young and fast," jeered the teenaged driver as he jumped out from behind the wheel.

The woman reversed, revved her engine, and rammed the Firebird. As the Mercedes reversed and headed for his car again, the teenager turned and gaped, then ran over and banged on the woman's window. "What the hell do you think you're doing?" he screeched.

She smiled sweetly and explained, "You've got to be old and rich."

•

Hear about the old queen who was brought up on charges of having molested a choirboy?

The judge dismissed the case on the grounds that the evidence wouldn't stand up in court.

•

Then there's the story of the elderly Italian gent who came in to see his doctor. He explained that he was thinking of marrying a considerably younger woman, and wanted the doctor's opinion as to whether he was sexually fit.

"Okay," agreed the doctor. "Let's have a look at your sexual organs."

"Here they are," said the old man, and obligingly stuck out his index finger and tongue.

Mrs. Garwood lived up in the hills and had always been healthy as a horse, but as old age approached, she found herself suffering from some "female troubles." Finally she confessed this to her daughter-in-law, who made an appointment with a gynecologist in the city and drove her in.

A wide-eyed Mrs. Garwood lay silent and still as a stone while the doctor examined her. When it was over, she sat up and fixed a beady eye on the physician. "You seem like such a nice young man," she quavered. "But, tell me, does your mother know what you do for a living?"

MISCELLANEOUS

When Alec was informed by his doctor that he had only twelve more hours to live, he rushed home and told his wife, who collapsed in racking sobs. But then she pulled herself together, clasped his hands in hers, and promised, "Then I'm going to make tonight the best night of your life, darling." She went out and bought all his favorite delicacies, opened a bottle of fine champagne, served him dinner dressed in his favorite sexy peignoir, and led him up to bed, where she made passionate love to him.

Just as they were about to fall asleep, Alec tapped her on the shoulder. "Honey, could we make love again?"

"Sure, sweetheart," she said sleepily, and obliged.

"Once more, baby?" he asked afterwards. "It's our last night together."

"Mmmhmm," she mumbled, and they made love a third time.

"One last time, darling," he begged a little later, shaking her by the shoulders.

"Fine!" she snapped. "After all, what do you care? *You* don't have to get up in the morning."

•

What's dumb?

Directions on toilet paper.

What's dumber than that?

Reading them.

Even dumber?

Reading them and learning something.

Dumbest of all?

Reading them and having to correct something you've been doing wrong.

•

This young couple decided to go for a drive in the country and soon found themselves way out in the woods, far from any town. Since they had both fantasized about making love in the middle of a road, and since this seemed as isolated a spot as they were likely to find, they pulled over, got out of the car, and began to go at it in the middle of the sun-warmed country road.

Not too much later a sixteen-wheeler came thundering around the bend. "Damn, that looks like two people buck naked in the middle of the road," muttered the driver to himself, and gave a few blasts on his horn, and then a few more. The squirming bodies—that's definitely what the obstruction was, the driver confirmed as he got closer—ignored the horn completely. Finally, the driver brought the huge truck to a screeching halt only a foot shy of the couple, who flopped onto their backs and smiled blissfully up at him.

"You damn fools coulda been killed!" yelled the driver.

"Didn't you see me coming? Or at least hear me coming?"

"Sorry, buddy," said the young man with a smile. "But I was coming, she was coming, *you* were coming—and you were the only one with brakes."

•

Read the new bestsellers?

"Fourteen Yards to the Outhouse" by Willy Makeit, (illustrated by Betty Wont),

"Fourteen Days in the Saddle" by Major Ashburn,

"The Hawaiian Princess" by Komoni Wonna Leia,

and the new Russian novel "Something is Missing" by Hubija Kokov.

•

"Doctor, Doctor," screamed the frantic young mother, "my baby just ate an entire tube of K-Y jelly! What should we do?"

Holding the receiver away from his ear, the doctor thought for a moment, then counseled, "Well, if you really can't wait, Parcells Drug is open all night."

•

Did you hear about the new restaurant that just opened up on the moon?

Good food, but *no* atmosphere.

•

An anthropologist had been studying an obscure Thai hill tribe when he contracted a particularly virulent case of jungle rot and was dead in a week. His heartbroken widow accompanied the casket back to Milwaukee, where she invited his three best friends to attend an intimate funeral. When the brief service was over, she asked each of the friends to place an offering in the casket, as had been the custom of the tribe he had been living with. "It would mean a great deal to Herbie," she said, then broke down into racking sobs.

Moved to tears himself, the first friend, a doctor, gently deposited one hundred dollars in the coffin.

Dabbing his cheeks, the second friend, a stockbroker, laid one hundred fifty dollars on the deceased Herbie's pillow.

The third friend, a lawyer, wrote a check for four hundred fifty dollars, put it in the casket, and pocketed the cash.

•

What's the difference between your paycheck and your wife?

You don't have to beg your wife to blow your paycheck.

•

This Yuppie went out and bought the BMW of his dreams, and as he was driving home from the dealer he decided to see what the car could really do. He was whizzing around a turn on a country road at about 80 mph when he hit an oily patch and skidded headlong into a telephone pole, totalling the car and nearly severing his wrist.

The next motorist on the scene screeched to a halt and rushed over to the car. Stunned, the driver was sobbing, "My car . . . look at my new car. . . ."

"Are you nuts, buddy?" yelled the passerby, pointing at the Yuppie's mangled arm. "Look at your *wrist*!"

"Oh, no," gasped the Yuppie, looking over and paling visibly. "My Rolex!"

•

Did you hear about the lawyer who was solicited to be a Jehovah's Witness?

She refused because she hadn't seen the accident, but said she'd be interested in taking the case.

•

After the annual office Christmas party blowout, Dawkins woke up with a pounding headache, cotton-mouthed, and utterly unable to recall the events of the preceding evening. After a trip to the bathroom he was able to make his way downstairs, where his wife put some coffee in front of him. "Louise," he moaned, "tell me what went on last night. Was it as bad as I think?"

"Even worse," she assured him, voice dripping with scorn. "You made a complete ass of yourself, succeeded in antagonizing the entire board of directors, and insulted the president of the company to his face."

"He's an asshole—piss on him."

"You did," Louise informed him. "And he fired you."

"Well, fuck him," retorted Dawkins feebly.

"I did. You're back at work on Monday."

•

How many directors does it take to screw in a light bulb?

None. Directors screw in hot tubs.

•

"Doctor Merrill," shrieked the nurse receptionist, bursting into his office. "You pronounced Mr. Van Heusen as healthy as a bull, and he just dropped dead outside the front door."

"Quick, Felice," ordered the doctor without missing a beat, "turn him around so it looks like he was coming *in.*"

•

Did you hear about the Texan who was so big when he died that they couldn't find a coffin big enough to hold the body?

They gave him an enema and buried him in a shoe box.

•

"Your Honor, Sir," explained the solemn young man who was next on the docket, "I'd like to get married."

"All right, all right. Your age, please?"

"I'm twenty-two, sir."

"And your wife-to-be? Where is she?" asked the judge, looking up from his papers rather irritably.

"Oh, she's right over there against the wall," said the young man, pointing in her direction, "and she's fifteen."

"Fifteen, eh? That's underage, young man—why, marrying you two would be against the law."

"I see," said the prospective bridegroom, a huge smile coming over his face. "Would you mind explaining that to the fellow next to her with the shotgun?"

•

The slovenly, obese Hollywood agent got up from his seat at the comedy club to go to the bathroom. Returning with Perrier and popcorn in hand, he inquired of a young woman, "Did I step on your foot a few minutes ago?"

"As a matter of fact, you did," she replied tartly.

"Great! Then that's my table."

•

McCain was outraged when his dentist's bill arrived in the mail, and lost no time reaching the office by phone. "It was just a simple extraction," he complained bitterly, "but you've charged me three times your normal rate."

"I had to," explained the dentist. "You made so much noise that two patients ran out of the waiting room."

•

"I'll never forgot the first time I turned to drink when women failed me," sighed the old wino to his buddy as they huddled in an alleyway.

"Oh yeah? How come?"

"Got my dick stuck in the neck of the bottle."

•

Houndslow had handled all of Harrington's legal affairs for years, and one day he had to make a difficult telephone call to his old acquaintance. Being a forthright type, he got right to the point. "Harrington, I have some terrible news and some really *awful* news."

The businessman sat down and disconnected the speakerphone. "Shoot, Houndslow."

"The terrible news is that your wife found a picture that's going to be worth several hundred thousand dollars," the lawyer informed him.

"That's the terrible news?" Harrington was intrigued. "I can hardly wait to hear the really awful news."

"It's a picture of you and your receptionist."

•

How did the bereaved family honor young Tom, who had died in the electric chair?

Every year they laid a wreath on the fusebox.

•

Little Janie went off to public school and came home full of questions. "Mommy, how did baby Brendan next door get born?" she asked.

"The stork brought him, honey," was her mother's prim reply. "Want to help me bake some cookies?"

"Nah. Mommy, so how did the twins in the corner house get born?"

"The stork just carried two babies at once, sweetie."

"Damn," muttered the little girl with a scowl. "Doesn't anyone in this neighborhood fuck?"

•

The psychiatrist closed his notebook, clasped his hands in satisfaction, and contemplated the patient sitting across from him. "I confess that in my profession one seldom speaks of 'cures,' Miss Kamin," he said sagely, "but at this time I am very pleased to be able to pronounce you one hundred percent cured. Goodbye, and good luck."

"Swell," muttered the woman, looking downcast and beginning to pout. "That's just swell."

The psychiatrist was taken by surprise. "Miss Kamin, I thought you'd be delighted. What on Earth is wrong?"

"Oh, it's fine for you," snapped Miss Kamin, "but look at it from my side. Three years ago I was Joan of Arc. Now I'm nobody."

•

Macrae and his wife saved and saved for a vacation in Rio de Janeiro, and they finally flew off. But on the third day he telephoned Doyle, his partner, to report that his wife had been injured in a car accident. "She's in a coma," Macrae reported, "so I'm gonna have to stick around for a few weeks till she can be moved."

"That's terrible—what're you going to do?" asked Doyle.

"Move to a cheaper hotel—what else?"

•

"Stanley, what are you cutting out of the paper?" asked Rhoda, who loved to pry.

"It's a story about a guy in Milwaukee suing for divorce because his wife kept going through his pockets," explained her long-suffering husband.

"Now Stanley, what on Earth are you going to do with a story like that?"

"Put it in my pocket."

•

"Tell me about you and your husband's love life," suggested the shrink.

"Well, it's like the Fourth of July," said the woman after a moment's reflection.

"Aha—you mean it's all firecrackers and emotional explosions?" pursued the doctor eagerly.

"No, no. I mean it happens once a year."

•

What do you call oral sex between Yuppies?

Sixty-something.

•

A rape victim, Marcella was mortified by the prospect of testifying against her attacker, but friends and family convinced her of her obligations. So the case came to trial, and at a certain point, the DA asked her what the defendant had said before the alleged assault. Blushing, Marcella requested permission to write out the answer rather than say it aloud. And after reading the note, the judge instructed that it be passed along to the members of the jury.

When the note reached the last juror, who was sound asleep, he was woken by an elbow from the woman next to him. She passed him the note, which read, "I'm going to fuck you like you've never been fucked before, sweetmeat." The juror grinned broadly, and slipped the note into his pocket.

"Will juror number twelve kindly pass the note back to the bench?" requested the judge.

"Oh, Your Honor, I can't," he stammered. "It's too personal."

•

"Tell me the truth, Doctor Hill," said the emaciated fellow. "How much longer am I going to live?"

"It's always hard to predict," she replied brightly, "but let's just say that if I were you, I wouldn't start watching any miniseries on TV."

TOO TASTELESS TO BE INCLUDED

What does the blinking neon sign above Frank's 24-Hour Abortion Clinic say?

"You Rape 'Em, We Scrape 'Em—No Fetus Can Beat Us!"

•

One night Lloyd and Lois were playing one of their favorite games in bed: fart football. Lloyd went first with a trumpeting fart. "Seven points," he declared proudly.

Lois's slightly less stentorian effort was only good for five, but within a few seconds Lloyd granted her the extra two points for pungency.

On it went, until the score reached 28–21, with Lloyd in the lead. Fiercely competitive, Lois strained and groaned until she was red in the face and until—to her considerable dismay—she shat right in the bed. She thought for a moment, then grinned and announced: "Halftime! Change sides."

•

"Mommy, Mommy, why is Daddy running back and forth across the field?"

"Shut up and reload!"

•

"Mommy, Mommy! Can't we give Daddy a decent burial?

"Shut up and keep flushing!"

•

"Mommy, Mommy, there's a mole on Grandma's leg!"

"Shut up and eat around it."

•

What do you do when you see six white guys beating up a black guy?

Laugh.

Then what?

Yell, "He raped my sister!"

•

What do you do when your baby dies on Thanksgiving Day?

Stuff the turkey with it.

•

What have you got when you cover four dead babies with a piece of glass?

A coffee table.

•

When they're piled on top of each other?

A stool.

•

What do you do with twin dead babies?

Use one to swat the flies buzzing around the other.

•

What have you got when you strap a dead baby to each foot?

Slippers.

•

A middle-aged divorcee, distraught at the thought of never having a baby, consulted doctor after doctor in vain. One, however, offered her the experience of what it felt like to be pregnant. She readily agreed, so he stuck a cork up her ass.

Three months later, the woman felt full but not full of

baby. After six months, she felt the same, only fuller. Nine months later she happened to be in the shower when a monkey who had escaped from the zoo came in the bathroom window, spotted the cork, and pulled it out. A giant brown explosion blew the woman off her feet and knocked her out. When she came to and set eyes on the monkey, she staggered to her feet and cried joyfully, "Sweetie, you may be brown and hairy, but you're all mine!"

Would you like to see your favorite tasteless jokes in print? If so, send them to:

Blanche Knott
c/o St. Martin's Press
175 Fifth Avenue
New York, N.Y. 10010

I'm sorry, but no compensation or credit can be given. But I *love* hearing from my tasteless readers.